The Unit Circle
is 2π's home.

It's a perfect home for him
because he is 6.28 units long.

For Thom, Pretoria and all the wonderful young people of MCPS and around the world who will learn to love Math with 2π

2 Pi Productions
902 Newhall Street
Suite 215
Silver Spring, MD 20901-3755

Copyright information available at Library of Congress
ISBN 978-0-9896108-0-3

Printed in the USA

Special Thanks to:
Sabrina McMillian, Lynn Camacho, Nicole Hoppman, Jennie Litvack, Jeannie Franklin, and Ari Antonelli for support
Dave Owens, Donna St. George, Kenya Young, Jo Reed, and Andrew Fullner for media exposure
Stephen Brown, Nick Pleasant, Ruth Warren, Gerald Carter, and Pretoria for design consulting
Chris Barclay, Dr. Joshua Starr, Renay Johnson, and MCPS for 17 wonderful years
Brad Holmes, Ruben Marbury, and Bob Millner for mentorship
Son Luc, Ernesto Lara, Rich Weinfeld, Steve Banvard
Chris Wells, and Peter Asch for partnership
Alan Meltzer, Jon Goodman,
Lance London , and
Valerie Ervin
for inspiration

Edited by Ruth Warren

2π Talks Math with the Queen of Honeytown

By

Mr. 2 Pi

It's 6:00 AM on the Unit Circle and 2π is ready for his morning walk.
Who will he meet today? What will he learn?

One day,
as 2π walked toward the Oak tree,
he looked up and noticed
Honeytown's Queen Bee.
Your highness, sorry to interrupt
the work on your hive,
but may I please have
a few minutes of your time?

Property
of
Honeytown, USA
Sure 2π, I will come down from the tree
and answer any questions that you have for me.

When bees construct their hives, how do they choose the shape?

Property
of
Honeytown, USA

We use hexagons to build our hives
because hexagons tessellate.

Only 3 Regular Polygons Tessellate

Regular Triangle

Regular

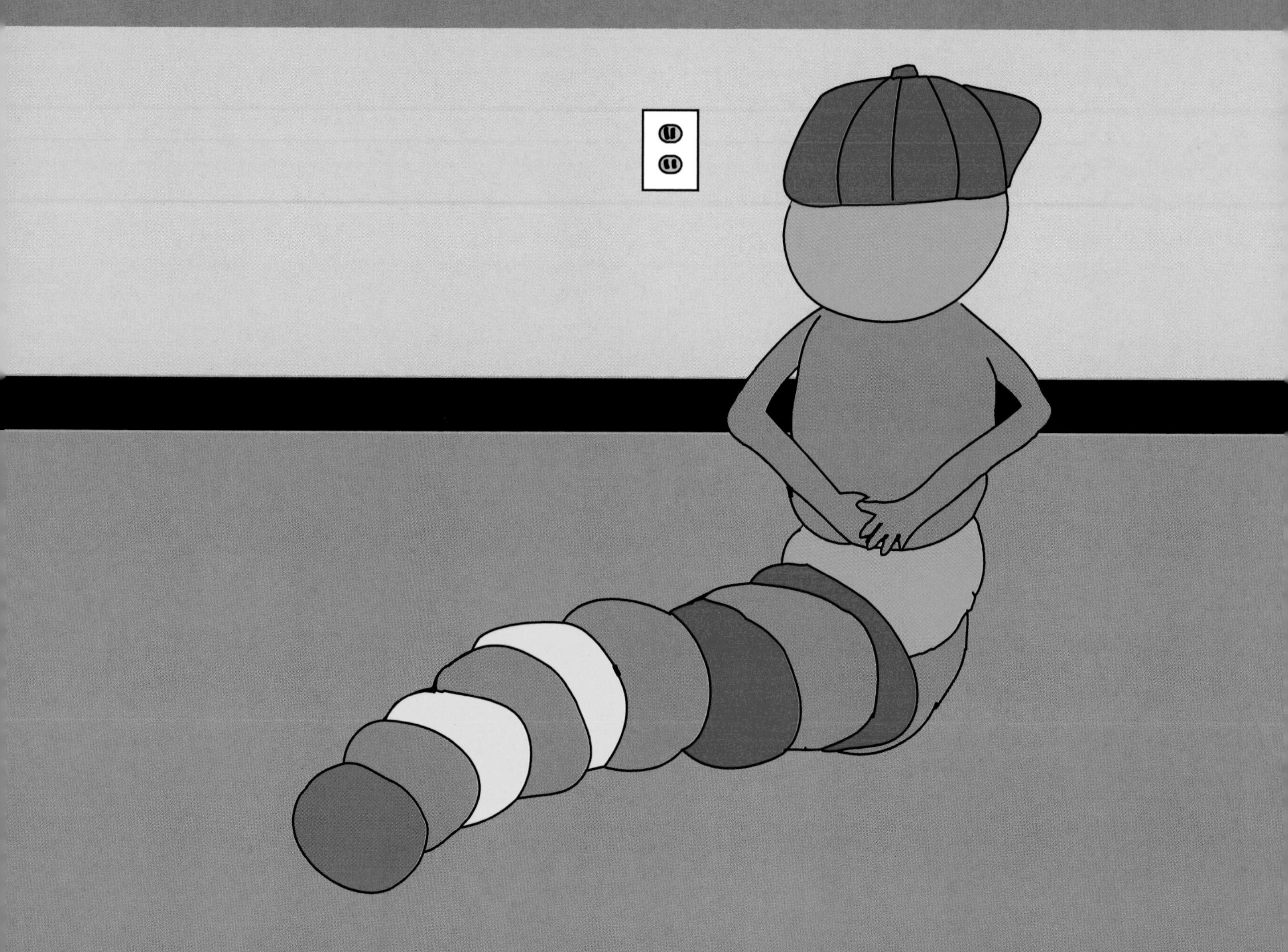

Vocabulary:

Regular Polygon - polygon with all sides and angles congruent.

Tessellate - To fit together perfectly without space in between.

Quadrilateral (Square)

Regular Hexagon

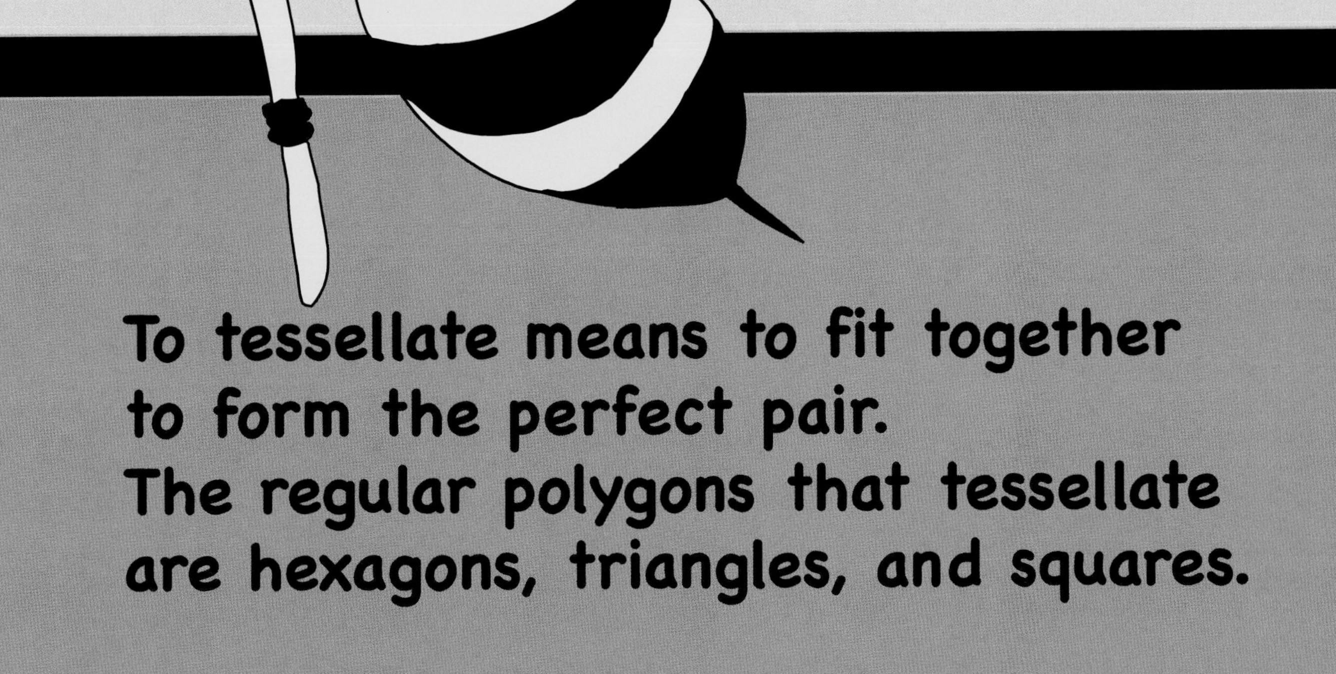

To tessellate means to fit together
to form the perfect pair.
The regular polygons that tessellate
are hexagons, triangles, and squares.

Only 3 Regular Polygons Tessellate

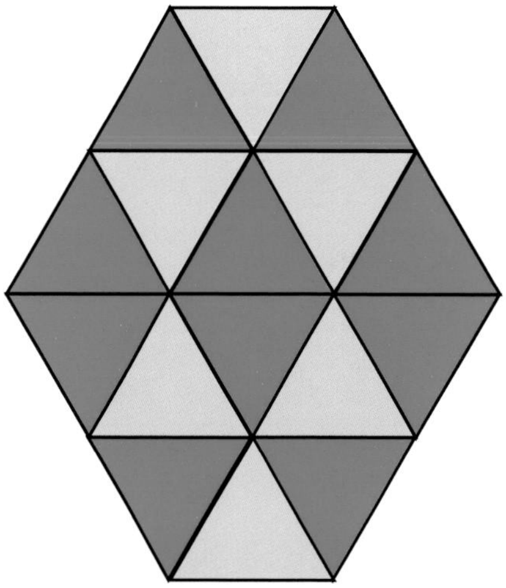

Regular Triangle

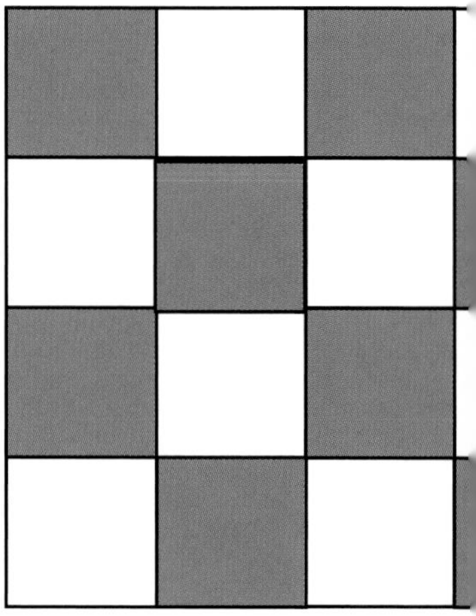

Regular

So, do some bees use triangles and squares to construct their hives?

Vocabulary:

Regular Polygon - polygon with all sides and angles congruent.

Tessellate - To fit together perfectly without space in between.

Geometry Class

It is very important that you know how to calculate the area and perimeter of each shape. For all regular polygons, area is half the product of the apothem and the perimeter. The perimeter is the sum of the sides.

Regular Triangle

Regular Quadrilateral

Regular Pentagon

Regular Heptagon

Geometry Class

When bees go to school, they study Geometry. There they learn how to build hives efficiently.

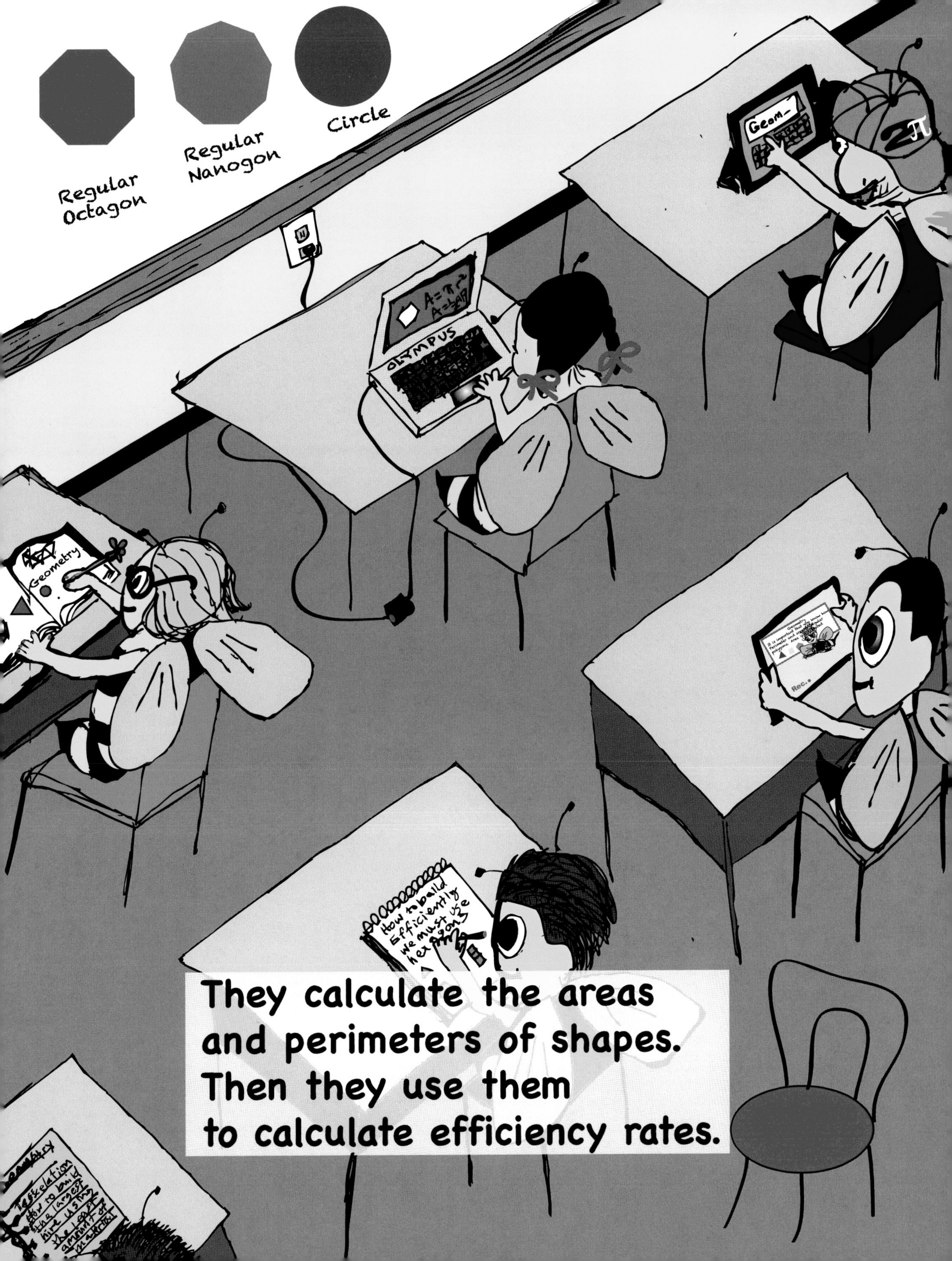

Regular Octagon

Regular Nanogon

Circle

They calculate the areas
and perimeters of shapes.
Then they use them
to calculate efficiency rates.

How do you calculate
the efficiency of a shape?

The area divided by the perimeter is the efficiency rate.

I prepared an exercise
to help demonstrate.
First, I constructed three polygons,
each with perimeter eight.
Next, I calculated their areas
using $\frac{1}{2}(a)(p)$.
Then, I divided each area by eight,
to find each shape's efficiency.

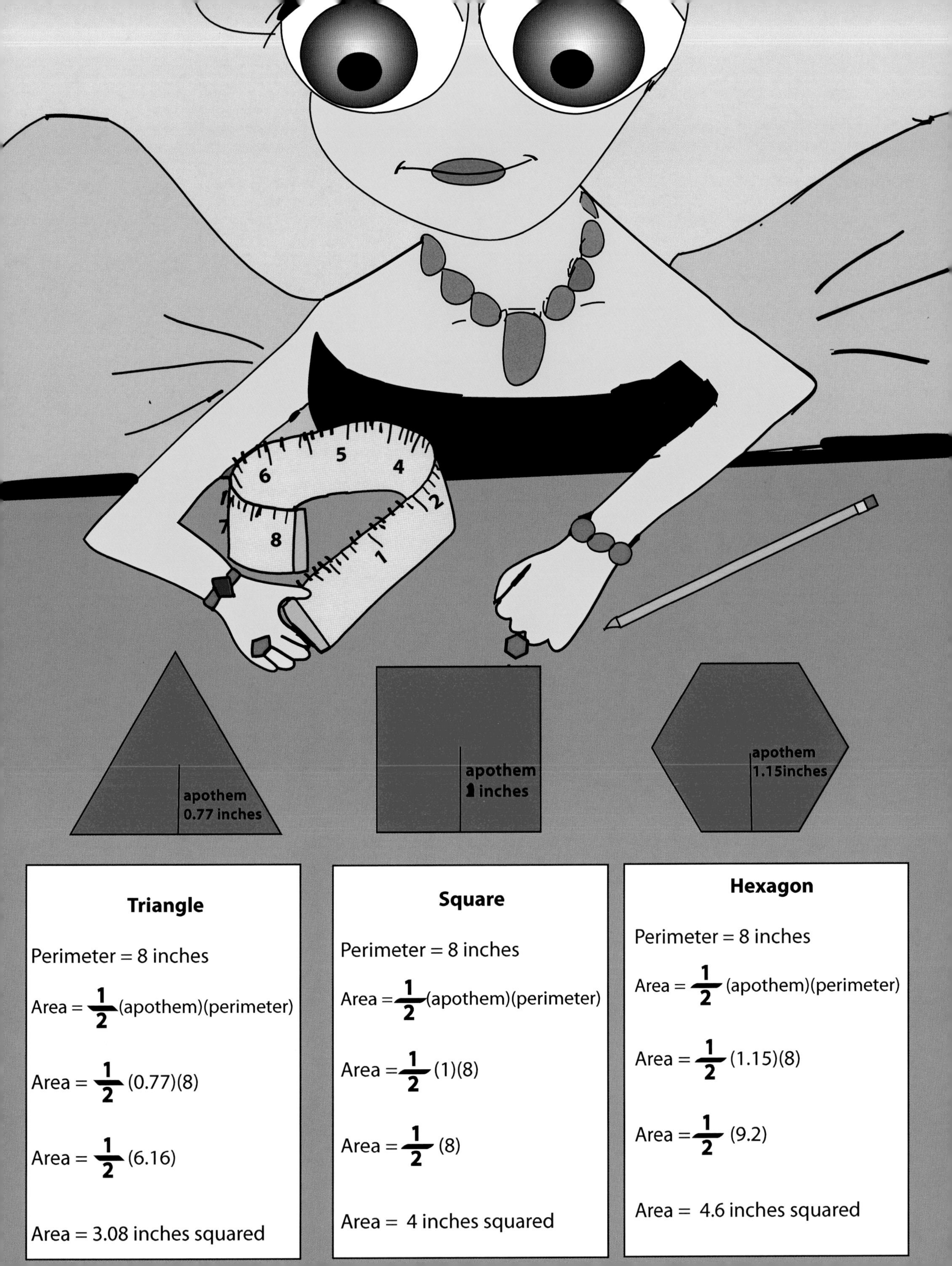

5
4
6
2
7
8
1
apothem
0.77 inches
apothem
1 inches
apothem
1.15inches
Triangle
Perimeter = 8 inches
Area = $\frac{1}{2}$(apothem)(perimeter)
Area = $\frac{1}{2}$ (0.77)(8)
Area = $\frac{1}{2}$ (6.16)
Area = 3.08 inches squared
Square
Perimeter = 8 inches
Area = $\frac{1}{2}$(apothem)(perimeter)
Area = $\frac{1}{2}$ (1)(8)
Area = $\frac{1}{2}$ (8)
Area = 4 inches squared
Hexagon
Perimeter = 8 inches
Area = $\frac{1}{2}$ (apothem)(perimeter)
Area = $\frac{1}{2}$ (1.15)(8)
Area = $\frac{1}{2}$ (9.2)
Area = 4.6 inches squared

Geometry Class

Regular Triangle

Efficiency rate = $\frac{3.08}{8}$

Efficiency rate = 0.385

Regular Quadrilateral

Efficiency rate = $\frac{4}{8}$

Efficiency rate = 0.500

Regular Hexagon

Efficiency rate = $\frac{4.6}{8}$

Efficiency rate = 0.575

Increasing the number of sides increases the efficiency rate.

Higher efficiency means a smaller amount of waste. In other words, which shape encloses the greatest space?

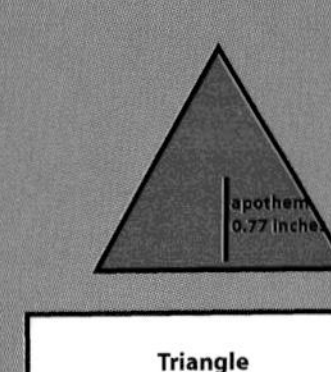

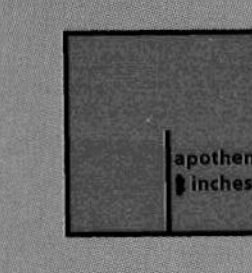

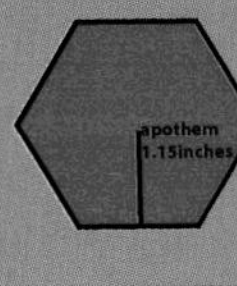

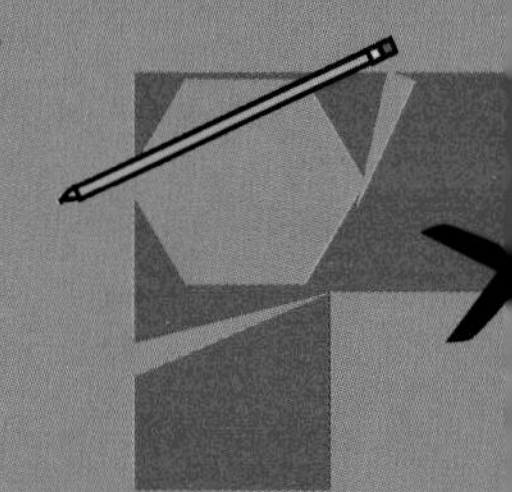

Triangle

Perimeter = 8 inches

Area = (apothem)(perimeter)

Square

Perimeter = 8 inches

Area = (apothem)(perimeter)

Hexagon

Perimeter = 8 inches

Area = $\frac{\text{(apothem)(perimeter)}}{2}$

Circle
A circle is not
a polygon because
polygons don't have curves.
Maximum
efficiency
= 0.637

Geometry Class

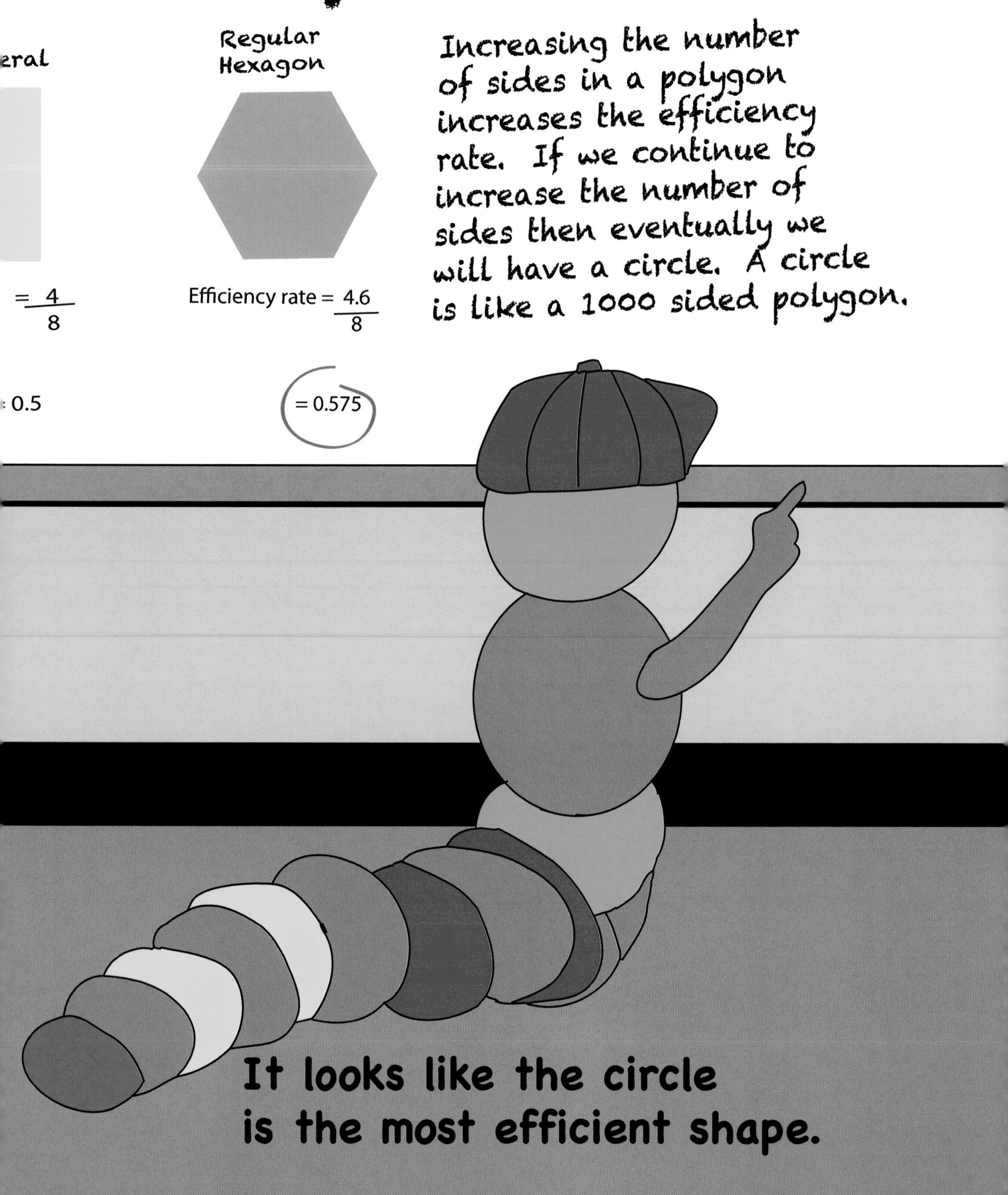

The circle is not a polygon because polygons don't have curves.
Circle
Maximum efficiency = 0.637
That's correct, 2π, but it does not tessellate.

Welcome to
Population: 1,359,256 Bees
Please don't text while flying.
Shop Safety Rules
1. Safety goggles at all times
2. Ear guards at all times
3. Fly slowly at all times
4. Keep the shop clean

Honeytown

When circles are stacked,
there are spaces in between.
If we had to fill those spaces,
that would slow our routine.
That would require more time,
more energy, and more material too.
The circle is a great shape,
but it doesn't work for what we do.

Shop Safety Rules
1. Safety goggles at all times
2. Ear guards at all times
3. Fly slowly at all times
4. Keep the shop clean
Honeytown
Mike's Broom
Shop room use only
RECYCLED WOOD

Of the three tessellating polygons from which we have to choose, the hexagon is the most efficient; so that's the one we use.

Thank you, your highness,
you've been extremely kind.
I appreciate what you shared
and I appreciate your time.

Property
of
Honeytown, USA

You are welcome, 2π.
The pleasure was all mine.
Honeytown loves visitors.
Come back anytime.

Talking Math with the queen
was such a wonderful time.
I should jot down some notes
while they're fresh in mind.

I learned that Bees use Math
to help construct their hives.
That's a great example
of Math improving our lives.

The Unit Circle is
2π's home.
60
45
30
0
Today, I had the
pleasure of meeting
the Queen of Honeytown.
She explained to me why
bees use hexagons to
construct their hives.
Bees use hexagons
because they are the
most efficeint shape of
the three polygons that
tessellate. The other
polygons that tessalate
are the triangle and the
square. The circle is the
most efficient shape of
all.

It's a perfect space for him because he is 6.28 units long.

Sweet dreams 2π...

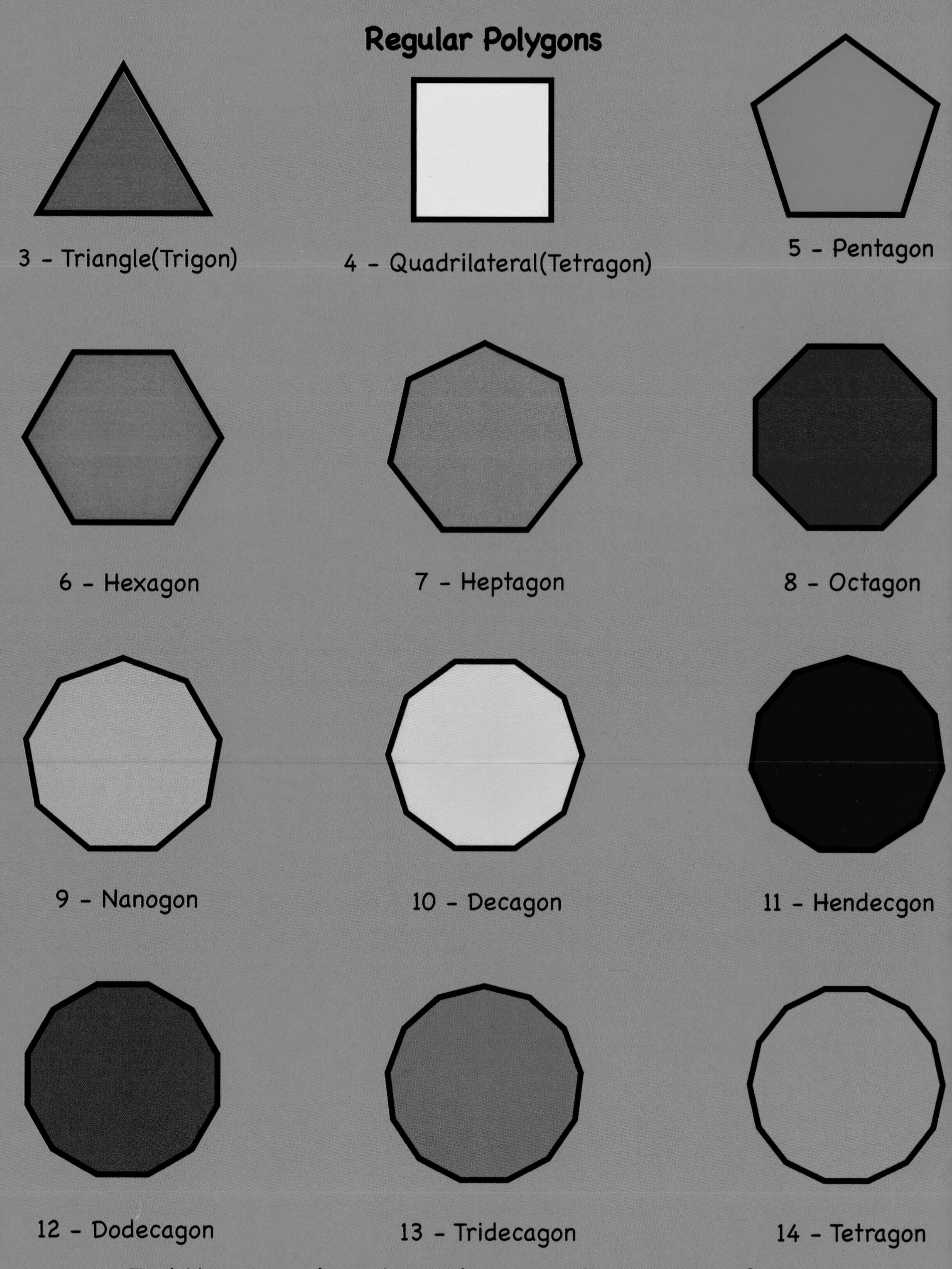

Test Your Learning: As we in crease the number of sides, the polygons are looking more and more like what shape?